DINOSAURS

Andrew Langley

W

FRANKLIN WATTS

Franklin Watts
338 Euston Road
London NW1 3BH

Franklin Watts Australia
Level 17/207 Kent Street
Sydney, NSW 2000

Series Editor: Amy Stephenson
Planning and production by Discovery Books Ltd
Editor: James Nixon
Series designer: D.R. ink
Picture researcher: James Nixon
Picture credits: Cover image: (shutterstock/DM7)

Getty Images: pp. 9 top (Jeffrey L Osborn), 11 (Craig Brown/Stocktrek Images), 14 (Dan Porges), 15 top and bottom (DEA PICTURE LIBRARY), 18 bottom (Craig Brown/Stocktrek Images), 19 top (DEA PICTURE LIBRARY), 27 top (Patrick Aventurier/Gamma-Rapho), 28 bottom (AFP). Shutterstock: pp. 2 & 12 (Kostyantyn Ivanyshen), 4 (Linda Bucklin), 5 (Catmando), 6 (Styve Reineck), 7 top (plena), 7 bottom (Computer Earth), 8 (Linda Bucklin), 9 bottom (JCElv), 10 (Catmando), 13 top (Leonello Calvetti), 13 bottom (DM7), 16 (DM7), 17 (Computer Earth), 17 bottom (Michael Rosskothen), 18 top (Linda Bucklin), 19 bottom (Linda Bucklin), 20 (Michael Rosskothen), 21 (Victor Habbick), 22 (Linda Bucklin), 23 top (Linda Bucklin), 24 top (Andrea Danti), 24 bottom (Dariush M), 25 top (Kostyantyn Ivanyshen), 25 bottom (Aaron Rutten), 26 (Relax Friday), 27 bottom (Jorg Hackemann), 28 left (Linda Bucklin), 28 middle-right (Marcio Jose Bastos Silva), 29 (Faiz Zaki). Wikimedia: pp. 9 middle (USDAgov/Flickr), 23 bottom (Mark Witton and Darren Naish).

Dewey number 567.9
ISBN: 978 1 4451 3598 4

A CIP catalogue record for this book is available from the British Library.
Printed in China

Franklin Watts is a division of Hachette Children's Books,
an Hachette UK company.
www.hachette.co.uk

CONTENTS

All words in **bold** can be found in the glossary on page 31.

There were many different types of dinosaurs. The *Spinosaurus* was a large meat-eater and had a skull like a crocodile.

WHAT IS A DINOSAUR?

Dinosaurs were the most successful animals that have ever lived. They ruled the Earth for more than 160 million years. That is a very, very, very long time. Compare that with the length of time humans have existed – just 200,000 years!

THE REPTILE FAMILY

The name 'dinosaur' comes from two words – 'dino' meaning 'terrifying', and 'saurus' meaning '**lizard**'. Dinosaurs belonged to the **class** of animals called **reptiles**. This includes creatures such as snakes, turtles, crocodiles and **iguanas**. Dinosaurs were land animals that formed their own group of reptiles – there were many different types.

TRUE OR FALSE?

Dinosaurs weren't lizards at all. **True or False?**

TRUE! Although many dinosaurs look like lizards, they belong to an entirely different group of reptiles.

We sometimes think of dinosaurs as huge, fierce monsters. Some of them were certainly very big, such as the *Sauroposeidon*, which weighed 60 tonnes. Its neck alone was about 12 metres long – nearly half the length of its body. Other dinosaurs were very small. One of the tiniest was the *Wannanosaurus*, which was only 60 cm long. Neither the *Sauroposeidon* or the *Wannanosaurus* were very fierce either, because they were **herbivores** (plant-eaters).

AMATING FACT
The biggest dinosaur?

The largest dinosaur identified so far is the *Argentinosaurus* (below). This monster was 37 metres long and weighed over 100 tonnes. But some scientists believe **fossils** found in India in the 1980s belong to something even more enormous – *Bruhathkayosaurus*. (Try breaking it down into: 'Bru – hath – kayo – saur – us'.) It has not been proven yet, but it is thought to have been 45 metres long, and weighed an incredible 200 tonnes (as heavy as two blue whales!). And in 2014 the fossils of seven enormous dinosaurs were found in the Patagonian desert in Argentina. They could possibly be the biggest dinosars ever found... so far.

DINOSAUR JOKE

Q How do you know if there's a dinosaur under your bed?

A Your nose is touching the ceiling!

A group of *Argentinosaurus* march across the landscape to find food and water.

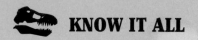

THE WORLD OF THE DINOSAURS

The rule of the dinosaurs began roughly 230 million years ago and lasted until about 65 million years ago, when they all died out. Today, there are no dinosaurs left alive (although many modern creatures, such as birds, are distantly related to them). All that is left are their fossils of bones and other remains, such as teeth and eggs, which have been found in most parts of the world.

AMAZING FACT
How many dinosaurs?

No one will ever know how many kinds of dinosaur there were. So far, scientists have discovered and named more than 700 different **species** of dinosaur. But scientists think that there was a much greater variety of dinosaurs on Earth. The remains of hundreds more new species are still waiting to be found.

Fossils of dinosaurs have been found all over the world. Scientists use these fossils to study what life was like millions of years ago.

TRUE OR FALSE?

One of the first dinosaurs to have lived was called 'a silly saurus'. **True or False?**

TRUE! although it was actually spelled '*Asilisaurus*'! It lived about 230 million years ago. It wasn't a monster – it measured just two metres long and probably ate plants.

MOVING CONTINENTS

Dinosaurs lived widely across the globe. How did this happen? The answer is simple: when the earliest dinosaurs appeared there was only one **continent**. All the dry land was joined together to form a single mass, which we now call Pangaea. This made it possible for all land creatures, including dinosaurs, to spread to almost every region.

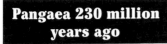

Pangaea 230 million years ago

200 million years ago

65 million years ago

Today

The Earth's **crust** is made up of a number of **plates**. During the dinosaur age, the giant continent of Pangaea began to break up. The plates drifted apart extremely slowly, eventually forming the continents of the world we know today (above). As they drifted, the dinosaurs and other animals were carried with them. The plates are still moving very slowly today.

This diagram shows how the continent of Pangaea has taken 230 million years to break apart into the continents on our planet today.

DESERTS AND SWAMPS

The world of the dinosaurs was very different from ours. During this time, most of the land was far from the sea, so there were vast stretches of desert. But, as the single continent began to break up, new environments were created – longer shorelines, **lagoons** and swampy forests. New types of trees and flowering plants developed, providing a wider choice of food.

Dinosaurs including *Triceratops* gather around a lake at the edge of the forest.

WHAT DID DINOSAURS LOOK LIKE?

Dinosaurs were **tetrapods**. This means they had four **limbs**, which they used to move about. Some dinosaurs used all four of their limbs for walking and running, while others just used their back limbs. Many other animals are tetrapods, including birds (whose front limbs have become wings) and of course humans (whose front limbs have become arms).

Many plant-eating dinosaurs such as this *Ampelosaurus* had small heads compared to their giant bodies.

AMAZING FACT
The brainiest and the dimmest

Lots of dinosaurs had really tiny heads. The smartest dinosaur was the *Troodon*, a small, bird-like dinosaur. It had the biggest brain for its body size of any dinosaur. The least intelligent was probably one of the early sauropods (see page 10), such as the *Sellosaurus*, which had a tiny brain compared with its enormous body.

MEAT OR VEG?

Most dinosaurs were plant-eaters, or herbivores. They ate leaves, shoots, fruits and other parts of the huge variety of plants available. The bigger the dinosaur, the more food it needed. Other dinosaurs were meat-eaters, or **carnivores**. They could chase dinosaurs and other prey, such as lizards and small **mammals**, quickly on two legs.

TRUE OR FALSE?

Plant-eating dinosaurs ate grass. True or False?

FALSE! They couldn't eat grass – for the simple reason that it did not exist so long ago. Grass plants **evolved** long after dinosaurs had disappeared.

PARTS OF A DINOSAUR

SKIN

The skin was leathery and scaly, like a modern-day crocodile's. It had to be tough to stop the dinosaur's body drying out in the hot Sun and to protect it from attack.

TEETH

Meat-eaters, like the speedy *Ozraptor*, had sharp teeth with **serrated** edges – perfectly suited to tearing flesh.

The vicious *Masiakasaurus* had sharp teeth that were perfect for grabbing and tearing up prey.

This tooth from a *Tyrannosaurus rex* was found in South Dakota, USA, in 2012.

Plant-eaters, like the *Apatosaurus*, had big spoon-shaped teeth, which they used for stripping leaves off trees. A few dinosaurs, such as the bird-like *Gallimimus* (left), had no teeth at all.

Gallimimus

LEGS AND FEET

The legs were positioned directly under the body. This allowed some dinosaurs to walk on their back legs. (Most other reptiles have legs that stick out at the sides of the body, which makes them waddle).

Big, heavy herbivores needed strong, thick legs to support their body weight. Their toes had short, sharp claws at the ends to help them grip in muddy places. Smaller carnivores had long legs and slim feet, which made them faster runners.

TAIL

Dinosaurs used their heavy tails for balance. A tail helped a two-legged dinosaur to walk and run and a four-legged dinosaur to stand upright on its back legs.

DINOSAUR JOKE

Q What do you call a sleeping dinosaur?

A A dino-snore!

PLANT-EATERS

Ask someone to describe a dinosaur. They'll probably use the words 'enormous', 'long necks', 'heavy' and 'slow'. There were certainly a lot of dinosaurs like this, with huge bodies and thick legs. They plodded across the landscape on all four feet. These creatures were plant-eaters, and they were the biggest of all the dinosaurs.

LIZARD-FOOTED DINOSAURS

The real giants of the dinosaur world were the group called the sauropods, which included the massive *Argentinosaurus*. Sauropod means 'lizard-footed', because they had five toes on each foot, just like lizards (many other dinosaurs had only three).

The sauropods had long tails, and tiny heads on long necks. One of the longest of all was the *Diplodocus*, which could measure up to 40 metres long from nose to tail. Using its extra-long neck, the *Diplodocus* could feed on leaves from very tall trees.

AMAZING FACT

The smallest dinosaurs

Some dinosaurs were the size of a chicken. One of the smallest ever found was the *Parvicursor* (meaning 'little runner' in Latin), which measured just 30cm from nose to tail.

A huge *Diplodocus* munches on the leaves of a tree.

DUCK-BILLED DINOSAURS

The hadrosaurs were one of the most common kinds of dinosaurs in the second half of the dinosaur age. They moved on all fours, but their front legs were shorter than the back ones. The most amazing thing about hadrosaurs was the long, flat beak on the front of the face (like a duck's bill). It was used for digging roots and other food out of the ground.

TRUE OR FALSE?

There's no such thing as a *Brontosaurus*. **True or False?**

TRUE! The name *Brontosaurus* was given to a newly discovered species of sauropod in 1879. Scientists later proved that it was not new at all, but actually an *Apatosaurus*. The *Brontosaurus* didn't exist.

Hadrosaurs such as these *Ouranosaurus* had wide, flat beaks for finding food in the ground.

GIANT DINO JOKE

Q What game does the Argentinosaurus most like to play?

A Squash!

THE MEAT-EATERS

The big, lumbering plant-eaters were easy to catch. So it's no surprise that they were hunted by carnivorous dinosaurs. These fierce hunters were **theropods** (which means 'beast-footed'). They moved fast on their hind legs, which had three toes on each foot. To grab their prey they used their incredibly strong jaws.

T-REX JOKE

Q Why did the Tyrannosaurus rex cross the road?

A Because chickens hadn't evolved yet!

Theropods such as this *Monolophosaurus* could run fast on their hind legs to chase their prey.

AMAZING FACT
The fastest runner

We can never know exactly how fast dinosaurs could move, there is simply no record of this. However, scientists believe the fastest runner of all was the *Dromiceiomimus*. This was a bird-like animal, similar to the modern ostrich. Scientists believe that *Dromiceiomimus* was an omnivore that ate both plants and meat. It had very long legs in proportion to its body, and could have reached over 70 kph (43 mph).

AMAZING FACT
Deadly claws

Some bird-like dinosaurs, such as *Deinonychus* and *Velociraptor* (see page 28), had huge, curving claws on their second toes. These were deadly weapons that could be used for slashing at an enemy. The claws could also pierce a victim's throat or pin prey tightly to the ground so the dinosaur could eat it alive!

FIERCEST OF ALL

The most famous meat-eating dinosaur was *Tyrannosaurus rex*. It was one of the largest and most ferocious of the theropods, as tall as a house and heavy as an elephant. A *Tyrannosaurus rex* could also run at speeds of nearly 20 kph (12 mph) – not super fast, but quicker than most of its prey.

A T-rex hunts a pair of *Gallimimus* running in the water.

T-rex probably had the most powerful bite – ever! Scientists have recently worked out that its jaw could crush with a pressure that was nearly twice as powerful as a crocodile's jaw, and 28 times stronger than a human's. They also had a huge array of lethal teeth. Some teeth were straight, others curved backwards to grip their prey, but all of them were very sharp.

TRUE OR FALSE?

The most expensive dinosaur **skeleton** is called Tyrannosaurus Nigel. **True or False?**

FALSE! It's actually called Sue. In 1990, **palaeontologist** Sue Hendrickson discovered an almost complete skeleton of a *T-rex* in South Dakota, USA. Nicknamed Tyrannosaurus Sue, the skeleton was sold to a museum in Chicago for $7.6 million – a record for a dinosaur fossil.

OUT OF THE EGG

How were dinosaurs born? Most babies hatched from eggs laid by females – just like reptiles and birds today. We know this because scientists have discovered fossilised dinosaur eggs in many parts of the world. They have even been able to identify what kind of dinosaur laid them, by **analysing** traces of chemicals in the fossils.

NEST IS BEST

Some mothers simply laid their eggs in hollows dug into the ground. Others built proper nests with raised edges of mud, and a few even lined them with twigs and ferns to make them more cosy. The bigger the dinosaur, the bigger the nest. Duck-billed dinosaurs laid their eggs in circular nests about three metres across.

TRUE OR FALSE?

The biggest dinosaur egg ever found was over 60 cm wide. **True or False?**

FALSE! No one has ever discovered one this big. Even so, scientists think that real giants, such as titanosaurs, may have produced eggs this large.

This reconstruction shows dinosaur babies hatching from their eggs in a nest made from raised mud.

A *Protoceratops* defends its nest from a dangerous predator that is trying to steal its eggs.

HATCHING EGGS

How did dinosaurs hatch their eggs? Big dinosaurs were too heavy to sit on their eggs without squashing them. They may have left them to be **incubated** by the heat of the Sun. Smaller dinosaurs were light enough to sit on their eggs and keep them warm. In Mongolia, fossil hunters found the skeleton of an *Oviraptor* mother with her feathers spread out to cover her eggs.

AMAZING FACT
Turning up the heat

The *Maiasaura* (which means 'caring mother lizard') worked out a clever way of looking after her eggs. She lined the nest with leaves and other plant material. This produces heat when it rots down and gives off enough warmth to help the eggs hatch out.

A *Maiasaura* watches her young as they begin to hatch out.

DAILY LIFE

Dinosaurs spent their days looking for food. This was a full-time job – especially if they had to compete with a lot of other dinosaurs. The herbivores had to find and eat huge amounts of plant material to fill their massive stomachs. The carnivores had to hunt and catch other animals or they would go hungry.

A gang of *Monolophosaurus* surrounds its prey – an *Einiosaurus*.

AMAZING FACT
The longest name

Some dinosaurs have long and confusing names. The longest and most confusing name of all has 23 letters in it! This creature is called *Micropachycephalosaurus* (try breaking it down into: 'Micro – pachy – cephalo – saurus'), which means 'tiny lizard with a thick head'. Fossilised bones of this dinosaur were dug up in China in 1978.

PREDATORS AND PREY

Even if they got enough to eat, many dinosaurs still had one big problem – how to stay alive. The plant-eaters were always under threat from the flesh-eating species. Big, savage beasts like the tyrannosaurs might **ambush** them, or they might be surrounded by packs of smaller hunters, such as *Deinonychus* and *Monolophosaurus*. To protect themselves, some herbivores lived together in large herds.

By living in large herds dinosaurs could defend themselves against attacks.

KEEPING WARM

Scientists used to think that all dinosaurs were **cold-blooded** animals, just like snakes and other reptiles are today. By using the heat from the Sun they warm up enough to be able to move about during the day. But now it seems some dinosaurs were warm-blooded – like birds today – and were able to keep a constant body temperature.

TRUE OR FALSE?

Dinosaurs could not actually roar like they do in films.
True or False?

TRUE! We will probably never know exactly what kind of noises dinosaurs could make. This is because any fleshy bits that would have helped make sounds have rotted away. But it seems unlikely they could create a loud and terrifying roar because they didn't have **vocal cords** in their throat. Scientists think some dinosaurs may have been able to make hooting noises by blowing air through their thin bony **crests**.

It is unlikely that dinosaurs could roar loudly – even fierce species such as this *Giganotosaurus*.

DINOSAUR JOKE

Q What do you get when two dinosaurs collide?

A Tyrannosaurus wrecks!

HORNS AND ARMOUR

Many plant-eating dinosaurs were slow. You might think this would make them easy for the carnivorous hunters to catch and kill. But this wasn't always true. Sauropods such as *Diplodocus* could use their enormous size to defend themselves. If they reared up on their back legs, they could threaten attackers with their front feet.

FIGHTING BACK

Some dinosaurs developed even better ways of defending themselves. Dinosaurs such as *Styracosaurus* (below) and *Triceratops* had forward pointing horns on their heads, and huge bony frills around their necks.

Stegosaurus

The *Stegosaurus* (above) had bony plates on its back and tail. It could use its powerful tail as a weapon by lashing it at an enemy.

AMAZING FACT
Bullet-proof dinosaurs

Scientists have discovered that some dinosaur armour was constructed in the same way as modern bullet-proof vests. The armour plates were made from layers of a fibre called **collagen**, which gave it great strength. It is a bit like the **synthetic** fabric called Kevlar® we use in bullet-proof clothing today.

In a fight *Styracosaurus* could use their hard frills for protection and thrust their horns into their enemy.

The *Ankylosaurus* (left) was the best armoured of all. It had ovals of bone fixed into its thick skin, short pointed horns on its head, and a massive club-shaped lump on the end of its tail.

TRUE OR FALSE?

The *Ankylosaurus* had eyelids made of bone. **True or False?**

TRUE! An *Ankylosaurus* was so well armoured that even its eyes were protected by bony lids.

DINOSAUR JOKE

Q What did the *Triceratops* sit on?

A Its tricera-bottom!

RUNNING AWAY

Some species of dinosaur had no armour or weapons to fight with, but had a different advantage over the carnivores – they could run faster than most of them. For example, *Orodromeus* and *Mononykus* were small and light with strong legs. *Orodromeus* means 'mountain runner' in Greek, and it could probably outpace most big carnivores.

These *Mononykus* dinosaurs were only a metre long, but could run at very high speeds.

SWIMMING SAURIANS

Imagine a sea monster. It's gigantic and dark-coloured, with a long, snaky neck and huge flippers. Over 150 million years ago, you could have seen a monster like this. The seas, rivers and lakes were rich with food, so it's no surprise that reptiles developed ways of hunting in water.

ICHTHYOSAURS AND PLESIOSAURS

Water reptiles included turtles and early forms of crocodiles. But the most successful were the ichthyosaurs (or 'fish lizards'). They were super-fast swimmers and skilled hunters. They chased small fish and other prey through the water, grabbing them with their spiky teeth. Ichthyosaurs had **streamlined** bodies, much like today's sharks or dolphins.

AMAZING FACT
The Attenborosaurus

As a boy, TV wildlife presenter Sir David Attenborough was fascinated by dinosaurs and plesiosaurs (see page 21). In 1993, he was honoured by having a newly discovered fossil of a plesiosaur named after him – the *Attenborosaurus*. Sir David has also had his name given to a species of tree, a shrimp, a spider and a carnivorous plant!

Ichthyosaurs looked like dolphins. They first appeared around 245 million years ago and lived up until about 90 million years ago.

Plesiosaurs (below) were the giants of the seas. Some were over 13 metres long, and weighed more than 25 tonnes. The largest species of plesiosaurs, such as *Kronosaurus*, were as big as a present-day whale. These huge creatures could not leave the sea, because the water supported their huge body weight. On land, they would probably have been unable to move!

TRUE OR FALSE?

Plesiosaurs still exist – and the most famous is the Loch Ness Monster. **True or False?**

FALSE! First of all, plesiosaurs died out with the dinosaurs (even though some people believe a few survived and lived in remote parts of the oceans). Secondly, if the Loch Ness Monster existed (unlikely!), it couldn't be a plesiosaur. These reptiles had to come to the surface to breathe – making them pretty easy to spot.

HOW DID PLESIOSAURS SWIM?

As plesiosaurs **adapted** to life in the sea, their limbs evolved into flippers. How did they use them to speed through the water? At first, scientists believed they swept the flippers back and forth (like we do when we swim). But now they think the reptiles flapped their flippers like wings, so they 'flew' underwater. Because they were air-breathing reptiles, they could not stay underwater for long, and came to the surface to fill their lungs.

The *Pteranodon* was one of the largest pterosaurs with a wingspan over six metres long.

FLYING REPTILES

The first creatures to fly were insects. But about 200 million years ago they were joined in the skies by something much bigger. This was the first pterosaur, or 'lizard with wings'. As they developed, these reptiles were able to fly faster, further and higher. This meant they could search more widely for prey – and swoop down on it from out of the blue.

MASTERS OF THE AIR

What made these early fliers so special? How did their bodies adapt to life in the skies? Here are some of the major features:

WINGS
Pterosaurs had huge flaps of skin connecting the sides of their bodies to a very long finger on each hand. These acted as wings.

STREAMLINED BODY

A slim body and thin, wedge-shaped head and mouth allowed pterosaurs to cut through the air with little **resistance**.

LIGHT WEIGHT

A pterosaur's relatively small body, which contained many hollow bones, was light enough to make flying and soaring possible.

EXTRA-SHARP EYES

Pterosaurs had to have keen eyesight to spot tiny land creatures or fish far below.

TRUE OR FALSE?

Modern birds are descended from pterosaurs. True or False?

FALSE! The real **ancestors** of birds were actually land-based dinosaurs, and not flying reptiles. These dinosaurs were probably quite small and had developed feathers. The most famous fossil of a feathered reptile yet discovered is the *archaeopteryx*, often seen as a halfway stage in the development of a dinosaur into a bird.

Archaeopteryx

The giant *Quetzalcoatlus* had a long neck and a large pointed beak, but no teeth. This picture shows *Quetzalcoatlus* feeding on the ground.

AMAZING FACT
Winged whopper

Quetzalcoatlus, discovered by fossil hunters in Texas in 1971, was named after the Aztec bird-god, Quetzalcoatl. It is the biggest flying creature ever found, with a wingspan of over 11 metres – that's even bigger than some small aircraft. Scientists have calculated that *Quetzalcoatlus* was able to fly at speeds of over 130 kph (80 mph) for as long as a week at a time!

THE GREAT EXTINCTION

A big meteorite crashing on the surface of Earth could have wiped out the dinosaurs.

The fire and dust created by a giant meteorite impact would cause havoc on Earth.

So how and why did the dinosaurs become **extinct**? About 65 million years ago something happened which killed off all the dinosaurs. Events like this are called mass extinctions. Nobody knows for sure what happened. And there is an even bigger mystery. Why did so many other creatures – mammals, fish, birds and plants – survive this disaster?

POSSIBLE ANSWERS:

A MONSTER METEORITE

Perhaps a massive chunk of rock (meteorite) from space hurtled to the Earth, causing shock waves, explosions and fires. Vast clouds of dust then blocked out sunlight, causing plants to die. The herbivorous dinosaurs starved, followed by the carnivores.

AMAZING FACT
Meteorite impact

We don't know for certain that a monster **meteorite** (above) caused the extinction of dinosaurs. But we do know that a giant meteorite struck the Earth at around the same time as the dinosaurs started to die out. You can still see part of the massive hole it made, measuring 180 kilometres across. Unfortunately, most of the crater is at the bottom of the sea, off the coast of Mexico.

The dinosaurs may have died out if the Earth got too cold.

A TEMPERATURE CHANGE

The Earth's climate may have cooled down. Dinosaurs and other big reptiles had no shelters, and no protection against the cold (unlike many smaller animals). Or maybe the climate got hotter, and many kinds of plants stopped growing.

TRUE OR FALSE?

The death of the dinosaurs was not the first mass extinction to occur. **True or False?**

TRUE! Way back in time, about 265 million years ago, there had been another disaster, which wiped out about 70 per cent of all the land animals. This left the world open for a new kind of animal to take over – the reptiles called archosaurs. And archosaurs developed into – you've guessed – the first dinosaurs!

A VOLCANIC ERUPTION

A series of enormous **volcanic eruptions**, bringing rivers of red-hot **lava**, smoke and fumes, could have been just as catastrophic as a meteorite strike – with the same result – the extinction of the dinosaurs.

A SLOW DEATH

Most scientists now agree that the extinction of the dinosaurs was not a sudden disaster. It took a long time – perhaps as long as 200,000 years. The world was changing and perhaps the dinosaurs could not survive these changes, unlike the new species that were emerging.

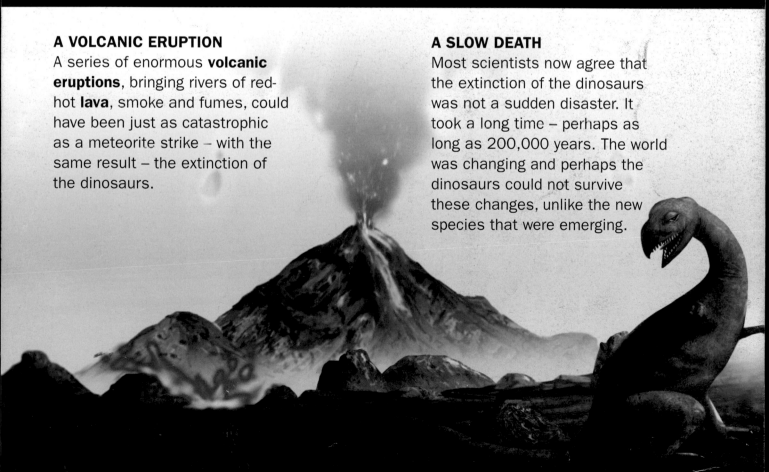

FINDING FOSSILS

Dinosaurs may be extinct, but they haven't disappeared altogether. Some of their remains can still be found scattered about the world, in the form of fossils. Most of what we know about the dinosaur age comes from these remains.

BONE BECOMES STONE

How does an animal become a fossil? Most of the dead dinosaurs just rotted away in the ground, first the flesh and then the bones. But a few of these bones were amazingly preserved, because of where a dinosaur died.

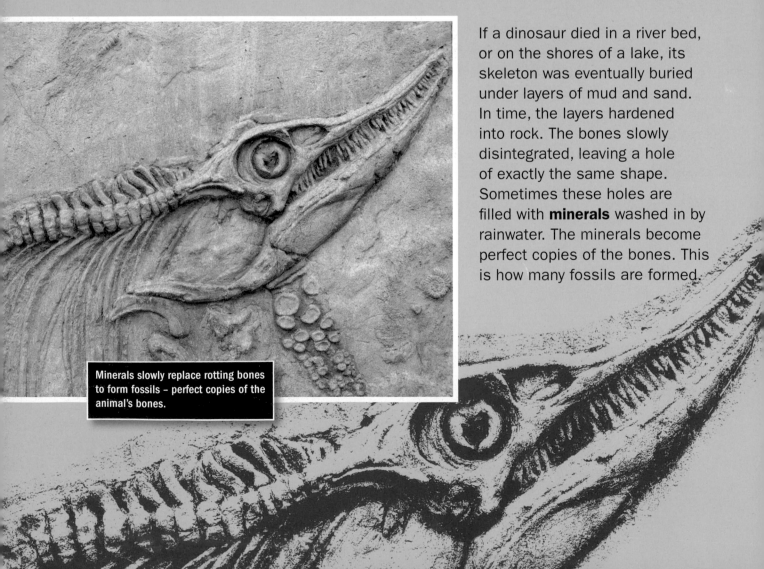

Minerals slowly replace rotting bones to form fossils – perfect copies of the animal's bones.

If a dinosaur died in a river bed, or on the shores of a lake, its skeleton was eventually buried under layers of mud and sand. In time, the layers hardened into rock. The bones slowly disintegrated, leaving a hole of exactly the same shape. Sometimes these holes are filled with **minerals** washed in by rainwater. The minerals become perfect copies of the bones. This is how many fossils are formed.

A fossil hunter discovers some dinosaur eggs in the earth.

REDISCOVERING THE DINOSAURS

Scientists who study the life of the **prehistoric** past are called palaeontologists (above). They go on fossil-hunting trips, and carefully remove the fossilised bones and other remains they find. Back in their laboratories or museums, the palaeontologists examine the fossils. They try to identify what kind of dinosaur the bones belonged to. Maybe it will be an entirely new species!

TRUE OR FALSE?

Most dinosaur skeletons you see in museums are made of plastic. **True or False?**

TRUE! Nowadays, the original fossils are rarely used to rebuild a display skeleton. Instead, **moulds** are taken from the fossils, and exact **replicas** are **cast**, using lightweight, plastic material.

AMAZING FACT
Accidental finds

A lot of fossil bones are found by accident, usually when the rock around them wears away or splits. One day in 1991 a lucky palaeontologist simply threw his rock hammer into a cliff in Colorado. Some rock fell away, revealing part of a *Stegosaurus* skeleton!

Museums display skeletons of dinosaurs that have been found across the world.

THE FUTURE

Imagine doing a jigsaw puzzle. Most of the pieces are missing – and what's more, you've got no idea what the final picture is supposed to be. Dinosaur research is a bit like that. Palaeontologists have discovered plenty of fossil remains, and identified several hundred species. But these are just a few of the millions of dinosaurs that must have walked the Earth long ago. There is still so much to find out.

The *Velociraptor* was a fierce, feathered dinosaur that lived towards the end of the dinosaur age.

WHAT NEW DINOSAURS WILL BE DISCOVERED?

One big area of interest are the feathered dinosaurs (above). Scientists now say there may be many more of these than they originally thought. And they could be discovered in places where they've never been found before, such as western Canada. Even more surprisingly, new finds may prove that *Tyrannosaurus rex* had feathers!

AMAZING FACT
Dinosaur City

Zhucheng in China is the site of the biggest and most astonishing fossil finds in history. Since 2008, palaeontologists have found:

• 7,600 dinosaur bones

• 3,000 fossilised dinosaur footprints

• thousands of fossil eggs

• the largest ever skeleton of a hadrosaurid (duck-billed) dinosaur.

A dinosaur footprint.

The excavations at Zhucheng will go on for many more years. No wonder it is known as 'Dinosaur City'!

Workers analyse thousands of bones at a patch of ground in 'Dinosaur City'.

WHAT NEW METHODS WILL PALAEONTOLOGISTS USE TO FIND OUT MORE ABOUT DINOSAURS?

Some scientists are developing robot dinosaurs, using exact replicas of fossil bones. They believe these can answer many of the questions fossils can't – such as: how did dinosaurs move?

COULD WE BRING DINOSAURS BACK TO LIFE?

It happened in the film *Jurassic Park*. Scientists recovered dinosaur **DNA** and used it to recreate these massive creatures. Could this be done in real life? Dinosaurs lived so long ago that none of their DNA has ever been found. As the dinosaurs' bones turned to fossils their DNA disappeared. But one day, as new technology is developed, it may be possible to grow a whole new dinosaur.

Could a *T-rex* be brought to life?

QUIZ

How much have you learned about dinosaurs from reading this book?
Here is a quiz to test your memory.

1. Were sauropods plant-eaters or meat-eaters?

2. What does the term 'tetrapod' mean?

3. What shape were dinosaur nests?

4. What do we call a scientist who studies dinosaur life?

5. How long ago (in millions of years) did the dinosaurs die out?

6. What did hadrosaurs use their hard 'duck's bill' for?

7. In which country is the site of the most fossil finds?

8. What was special about the *Dromiceiomimus*?

9. Which was the biggest species of flying dinosaur?

10. What class of animals did the dinosaurs belong to?

11. What is the scientific name meaning 'lizard with wings'?

12. How many horns did the *Triceratops* have on its head?

13. What kind of dinosaur was the *Attenborosaurus*?

14 What was the name of the single giant continent that existed when dinosaurs first appeared?

15. Did *T-rex* run on two legs or four?

AMAGING FACT
When did these reptiles appear?

Ichthyosaurs	appeared 245 million years ago
Pterosaurs	220 million years ago
Monolophosaurus	180 million years ago
Stegosaurus	156 million years ago
Diplodocus	155 million years ago
Archaeopteryx	147 million years ago
Ouranosaurus	115 million years ago
Spinosaurus	95 million years ago
Oviraptor	85 million years ago
Gallimimus	74 million years ago
Tyrannosaurus rex	67 million years ago
Triceratops	67 million years ago

GLOSSARY

adapt to adjust to a new environment or situation

ambush a surprise attack made from a hidden place

analyse look at in detail

ancestor an animal from which later animals are descended

carnivore an animal that hunts and eats the flesh of other animals

cast shaped by pouring into a mould

class a group of animals that share the same characteristics

cold-blooded describes an animal whose body temperature changes depending on how hot or cold the environment is

collagen a tough substance found in bone

continent one of the major land masses of the world, such as North America or Europe

crest a bony ridge on the top of an animal's head

crust the top layer of rock on planet Earth

DNA (short for deoxyribonucleic acid) a substance that can make copies of itself and carries information about the make-up of our body

evolve to develop very gradually into something different

extinct no longer existing because the species has died out

fossil the remains of an animal or plant that is preserved in rock

herbivore an animal that eats plants

iguana a large American lizard

incubate keep eggs warm to help them hatch

lagoon a lake of salt water separated from the sea

lava molten rock that comes out of a volcano

limb one of the jointed body parts of an animal or human, used for moving or grasping

lizard a type of reptile which has a long body and a tapering tail

mammal a type of warm-blooded animal, of which mothers suckle (give milk to) their babies

meteorite a fragment of rock from outer space that has landed on a planet

mineral a substance that occurs naturally in the ground

mould a form used for shaping a soft material

palaeontologist a scientist who studies fossils

prehistoric part of the time before recorded history

plate one of the pieces of the Earth's crust, which is constantly on the move very slowly

replica an exact copy of something

reptile a type of animal that has dry, scaly skin and lays eggs

resistance a force, such as the wind, that slows down movement

serrated having an edge with tiny teeth

skeleton the framework of bones that supports an animal's body

species a type of animal or plant: members of the same species can mate or pollinate and produce young or new plants

streamlined shaped so it can move through air or water easily, with little resistance

synthetic made using chemicals and not natural

tetrapod an animal with four legs and feet

theropod a carnivorous dinosaur with large back legs and small front limbs

vocal cords folds of tissue in the throat that produce sounds when they vibrate

volcanic eruption the ejection of lava and gases from a hole in the Earth's crust called a volcano

WANT TO KNOW MORE?

Here are some places where you can find out a lot more about dinosaurs:

WEBSITES

http://www.kidsdinos.com/dinosaurs-for-children.php
Contains information, games, maps and even noises.

http://www.kidsites.com/sites-edu/dinosaurs.htm
Lots of links to good dino sites.

http://www.nhm.ac.uk/kids-only/dinosaurs/
The junior site of London's Natural History Museum.

http://www.walkingwithdinosaurs.com/
Amazing videos, animations and information.

www.bbc.co.uk/nature/life/Dinosaur
A very wide-ranging and useful site.

BOOKS

Ankylosaur Attack: A Dinosaur Adventure, Daniel Loxton, (Franklin Watts, 2013)

Dinosaurs (It's Amazing), Annabel Savery, (Franklin Watts, 2013)

Dinosaurs! series, David West, (Franklin Watts, 2015)

Dinosaurs, Joseph Staunton, (Frankin Watts, 2012)

Prehistoric: After the Dinosaurs, David West, (Franklin Watts, 2014)

Prehistoric Safari series, Liz Miles, (Franklin Watts, 2013)

Website disclaimer:
Note to parents and teachers: Every effort has been made by the Publishers to ensure that these websites are suitable for children, that they are of the highest educational value, and that they contain no inappropriate or offensive material. However, because of the nature of the Internet, it is impossible to guarantee that the contents of these sites will not be altered. We strongly advise that Internet access is supervised by a responsible adult.

INDEX